Faith Millennium Generation

Handing on Pastoral Care and Worship to Young People

Steve Tash
Coventry Diocesan Youth Officer and
Priest-in-Charge, Salford Priors

Patrick Angier
Youth Minister, Bedworth Team Ministry

Paul Simmonds
Coventry Diocesan Mission Adviser and
Associate Minister, St Margaret's, Wolston

GROVE BOOKS LIMITED
RIDLEY HALL RD CAMBRIDGE CB3 9HU

Contents

1. What is the Problem? by Paul Simmonds 3
2. Who Are We talking About? by Steve Tash 7
3. Who is in Charge? by Patrick Angier 15
4. What Shall We Do Now? by Paul Simmonds 23

Acknowledgements
The extract from *Accompanying* by Maxine Green and Chandu Christian (Church House Publishing, 1998) is copyright © The Central Board of Finance of the Church of England and Chandu Christian 1998 and The Archbishops' Council and Chandu Christian 1999 and is reproduced by permission.

The Cover Illustration is by Peter Ashton

Copyright © Steve Tash, Patrick Angier, Paul Simmonds 1999

First Impression December 1999
ISSN 0144-171X
ISBN 1 85174 420 7

1
What is the Problem?

Recently when a vicar announced he was leaving, one eager parishioner trawled through the diocesan directory to look for a likely replacement. He was hoping to find someone in their thirties. He came away horrified to discover there were only a handful.

None of the authors of this book would have suited that parishioner. One is still in his thirties, but is an unordained youth minister. The other two are forty-plus and fifty-minus respectively…or should that be respectfully!

As the latter of these, and an enthusiast rather than a specialist in youth ministry, I want to outline some facts that have convinced me that we have an urgent task on our hands. I believe the two main chapters will then give you, as they have given me, a sense of hope. God is in the business of re-creation. We have perhaps a decade left to '*traditio*,' to hand on and hand over the faith to the next generation in an adequate way. There are some incredibly courageous pioneers among the under thirties around the country. Channel 4 spotted some of them in the Christmas '97 series about new youth churches. The Archbishop's 'Time Of Our Lives' weekend brought some of them into the limelight. But we have a long way to go and they need all the support we can give them. That is the purpose of this book. The three of us can only speak in detail about our own denomination, the Church of England, but we hope others will compare and contrast this with their situation—we certainly need to work together.

The Greying of the Clergy

Perhaps it would come as a shock to most people to discover that the number of professional ministers in their twenties is tiny, probably two per diocese. In fact if early retirement at 50 were to be offered now to all current parish clergy (as it is in parts of the USA), then the Church of England would stand to lose the majority of its front-line workforce. The situation in most of the other historic denominations is no better, I understand.

Because clergy are mainly older this can mean that young people get a raw deal for a number of reasons. 'Older' people have not got as much energy. They observe the youth culture but joining in is an effort because they do not spend all their life in it. When there is so much to do it seems easier to look after PLUs—'People Like Us'—which we do so much better. A number of well-resourced churches have recognized the need for professional ministry among the under-25s. They employ gifted young people to do this work but they often have little official recognition, status or job security. There has been a rapid growth in the number of these full time youth workers—in fact there are now more of them than there are curates.

How Did We Get Ourselves Into This Situation?

Two things influenced this development both of which seemed reasonable at the time. First, in about the 1970s, the idea took root that young curates, straight out of school and college, were simply unprepared for the needs of ministry which demanded someone with some 'experience of life' and so many young candidates for ordination were told to go away and get some.

When Bishop Michael Baughen (now retired) was Candidates Secretary of CPAS in the 1960s he was in his early thirties. He was considered 'experienced' and pioneered 'You and the Ministry Weekends' which still run several times a year to help people understand what is involved in being in the ordained ministry. Nowadays the average age of ordination in the Church of England is around 38! (In fact you cannot even be ordained into Local Ordained Ministry until you are 30!) During the 1990s, the number of over-fifties recommended for ordination has more than doubled while the number of under-thirties dropped by a third. Recent figures show a small increase in the number of younger candidates, but while encouraging this is frankly not sufficient. The recent increase in the budget for ordination training was mainly due to an increase in numbers of candidates who have left established careers and are well into their thirties. Very few would be candidates for the role of youth ministry. Most will not work long enough to receive a full pension from the church when they retire.

Second, in the last twenty years even those curates who had youth on their side often resisted the idea that they should do youth work simply because they were young. For some that was the only sort of ministry they had been allowed to do before training and now they wanted to stretch their wings. They also wanted, as quickly as possible, to be regarded as professionally trained to work with all age groups. Furthermore, Post Ordination Training invariably insists on a broad syllabus relating to all aspects of ministry.

Why Does it Matter?

We have now reached a position where only one in five parishes has any teenage work at all. Less than half have any children's work. Most thinking Christians, when they are told of this situation, regard it as a scandal.

It is one thing to be taken unawares; it is another to ignore the situation when it is brought to your attention. Many churches have begun to respond. A small proportion have dived into their pockets and appointed their own paid youth workers, but this is only an option for larger, richer churches.

WHAT IS THE PROBLEM?

Others who cannot afford this have reluctantly let their young people go elsewhere (rather than risk them abandoning their faith), often to livelier 'new' churches. This can have advantages in promoting church unity but it does not increase the number of young people drawn into Christ's kingdom—indeed, the opposite is more likely to be true.

The people who have suffered are the young people who could rightly claim that on the whole they have been left 'like sheep without a shepherd' (Matthew 9.36). They have been marginalized and ignored by their churches and denominations who do not seem to want them any more.

So one urgent task is to address the age profile of the professional leadership of the church. Equally challenging for the Church of England (and most mainline denominations) at the end of the second millennium is the age profile of the members.

Put simply it looks a bit like this:

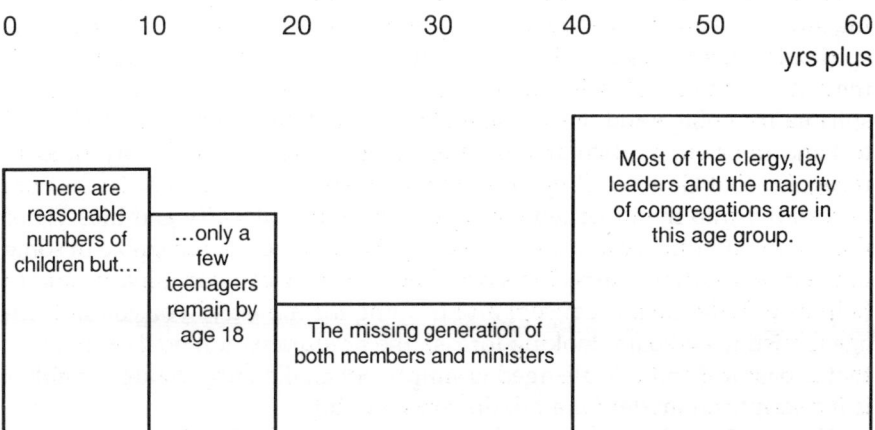

The Age Profile of the Congregations

One thing that has changed (for the worse) is the age when children stop attending. Many leave before they have had a chance to establish their own faith independent of their parents. Most churches find that it is increasingly hard to keep girls over 13 and boys over 8 or 9. It is equally hard to attract in older children and young people who have no church background.

Some justify this situation by claiming 'they'll come back later when they settle down and have kids of their own.' This may have been true to some extent in previous generations. But this is hardly a coherent youth strategy for building the church. It shows how desperate we have become that we grasp such straws. People cannot come back if they have never been and as we have seen 50% of parishes do not even have children's work!

It may not be very obvious at the moment but I am optimistic. Let us not be discouraged, but let us not hide our heads in the sand either. Let us face up to what is happening in this part of the church at this time. In the USA 35% of young people are part of a church youth group. Around the world, millions of young people are growing strong in faith. I do not want us to be discouraged, just honest. I know we have a senior leadership in the Church of England that is deeply concerned about the situation and yet believe that God still has a future for the church.

How would you have reacted as a youngster if all the ministers you knew were 'old'? (Remember that for most people under 25 anyone over 40 is 'old,' 'mature,' or even 'a crumbly,' and, in most cases, not naturally on their wavelength. If you doubt this, think back to when you were 25).

But there is a deeper cultural reason for the lack of young ministers. Speaking of potential young leaders, Paul Roberts comments, 'They have refused to follow the route into Christian leadership because they perceive a growing gulf between the agenda presently pursued by the wider church and the spiritual needs expressed within the culture of their peers. These needs, which they also find reflected in themselves, are not being met by the worship, spirituality, politics and mission agenda of mainstream church life.'[3] We need to hand over our particular model of being church. We probably need to recognize that God is calling young women and men into ministry but not necessarily into the inherited concept of both the authority and lifestyle of the ordained ministry as currently set up. Should we not recognize in some of the new youth workers God's prophetic voice to lead our thinking and to help us to redefine our concept and training for ministry? For young teenage Christians who are looking for risk the predominant model of ministry that is pastoral and middle-aged is simply not challenging enough. Neither is it a scriptural model for a missionary church.

When a 20+ adult from our church was accepted for ordination training last year my teen-age daughter was surprised. 'She's far too lively to be a vicar—she should be a youth worker.' Teenagers are more likely to respond to a demanding ministry in which to work and exercise faith, rather than a pew full of Grannies—they will realize how challenging that is later! The new 'Centre for Youth Ministry' is providing such opportunities and providing quality training. The candidates have few ambitions to wear grey suits and dog collars. They are very cool and missionary minded. However, whilst long-term youth ministry is right for some I suspect others are taking that route because it seems the only one open to them. If more bishops would ordain such young people specifically into youth ministry we would quickly have a revolutionized and vibrant new-looking sector of the Church of England, speaking the language of today's young people. If we do not take this matter seriously in the next decade it may well be too late after that.

2
Who Are We Talking About?

It is increasingly difficult to describe something called youth culture. This is not only because teenage attitudes stay with some people well into their sixties but also because the web is so vast and the choices are so wide. Tens of millions may watch the same 'soap' but the rest of their lives may be very different. One teenager likes carpentry, another reads Jane Austen. In a group of friends, three like fashion shopping, another prefers sport. Some like their music loud, some rarely listen to music. Others have no friends. Some feel alienated from the culture presented to them on TV. Many are not financially able to participate in the retail-induced culture of fashion and culture.

We therefore cannot create a perfect culturally appropriate style of worship or evangelism. None of our attempts to be like youth are wasted and we do need to be 'all things to all people' (1 Cor 9.22). But if we think that there is one thing called 'youth culture' we are simply stereotyping. We can try to be relevant and appropriate but will never catch all nor satisfy all. And we want to offer so much more than the retailer and the entertainer.

Cross Cultural Mission

Three things are vital in any attempt to reach across culture: a sincere willingness to listen; a deep reliance on God through prayer; and love.

The term 'listening' does not necessarily imply listening to someone's articulate conversation. A young person may find it difficult to explain their culture. Listening implies observing, studying, respecting and being willing to learn. Such listening will help an understanding of the culture and we will meet the real people behind the images. Listening will challenge our own cultural assumptions and prejudices. In listening, a real encounter can take place, which is fertile ground for the love and power of God.

Because our laudable attempts to be all things to all people will always be imperfect, prayer to the God who transcends cultural barriers, who removes our fear of other cultures and who can see the whole wonderfully complex picture of any culture, is essential.

Love speaks for itself and is eloquent witness to the God of love. Show me your culturally appropriate youth service with its expensive sophistication without love, and I will call it a clanging computer-enhanced gong. I know a teenager who, I was surprised to discover, on moving away from home, found a spiritual home in an evensong. He was loved.

1. Leadership and Worship

Part of our problem is that the church has become the provider of worship. In the main, young people are excluded from the production and composition of worship. This is especially endemic in the Church of England where liturgy and music have traditionally been the choice of the centre. Liturgy is provided. Clergy have to conform. Church music is the vicar's favourite hymnbook. Some reading this may regard it as a caricature, but it seems to me that priests and the institution still hold the power when it comes to the way worship is provided in many, many a parish.

Sadly this alienates those who have preferences for other music and lyrics. It excludes those who have gifts in leading worship. There is always fear in cross-cultural work. The unknown is frightening. So we fall back on what feels safe. We are unwilling to let the next generation shape the liturgy, the worship. We have locked it up in order to keep it safe. But the word '*traditio*' means to hand on. Our unwillingness to release the talents and gifts of young people impoverishes the church. The very inheritance we are supposed to pass on is not taken up by the next generation. We serve up, as year succeeds on year, a diet of worship which is farther and farther removed from that which young people would create, and so they do not absorb it or own it. Yet there is plenty of space even in our present liturgies to allow creative contributions from young people. I have personally found some music and lyrics from *Delirious?*, Matt Redman and Rebecca St James, very helpful for confession or commitment or praise during the services.

Lesslie Newbigin writes;

'If the gospel is to be understood, if it is to be received as something which communicates truth about the real human situation, if it is, as we say, to "make sense" it has to be communicated in the language of those to whom it is addressed and has to be clothed in symbols which are meaningful to them. And since the gospel does not come as a disembodied message, but as the message of a community which claims to live by it and which invites others to adhere to it, the community's life must be so ordered that it "makes sense" to those who are so invited. It must, as we say, "come alive." Those to whom it is addressed must be able to say, "Yes, I see."'

The Gospel in a Pluralist Society (SPCK, 1997)

Concern about worship is therefore not solely about style. It is also about who creates and who leads. The new culture of the Church of England needs to be about youth having real freedom to lead, coupled with accountability to older and wiser guides. I know very few youth mavericks disowning any attempt to be supervised. On the contrary, the cry from many youth workers is, 'Please manage us. Please give us proper accountability.'

WHO ARE WE TALKING ABOUT?

The fear that the new will inevitably erase the old overnight often hinders change. This is not necessary. New forms can co-exist alongside. We can have an 'as-well-as' rather than an 'either-or.' This is not about making clergy busier. It is rather releasing new leadership into the mission of discovering a new Church of England for a new culture.

As a young person in any family must be allowed to grow and develop beyond the boundaries of home and parents, so youthful leadership must be allowed to fully function—without being patronized! How far does any family progress if the parent figure does everything and makes every decision?

We fear fragmentation in the church through youth congregations. But a family does not fragment where there is love and freedom. The parent figure realizes that all members cannot look the same. Insistence on uniformity stifles. It is no good blaming the child for their rebelliousness when it is merely a product of overbearing authority.

Young people are worshipping together in so many creative ways across the whole country. Such worship is generally far more accessible to other non-church young people than traditional worship. So we need to encourage it and see it as both missionary into youth culture as well as valuable in feeding our present young Christians.

Like most vicars, I guess, I do not want to lose my teenagers from regular worship where we gain from them and they gain by relationships with older and younger Christians, but neither do I want to stop such exciting missionary ventures which clearly inspire and challenge them. I want to embrace their new worship within the Church of England and see it as part of the diet that this local church offers its varied population. People do move between services of course and in this way there is sharing of spiritual riches.

We need to give more freedom, trust and love for the youth in the Church of England. Then the whole family will grow, develop and remain a loving close family. The days of the vicar doing everything are over. The days of uniformity are numbered. The greying of the church needs to be reversed. Youthful leadership needs special encouragement and wants wise accountability and spiritual guidance. The new Church of England family will grow when we stop insisting new ventures of faith must look like the old Church of England. Bishop Michael Marshall said at a recent conference, 'the cloth is unravelling and a patch will not help. We need new looms to weave new cloth.' I would add that we need young weavers too.

New Looms; New Weavers

Many church leaders have been providing the equipment for new looms and the encouragement for new weavers for years. Now we need more and more adults who will enable young people to cross cultural barriers with the message of God's love rather than simply take the intercessions, preach a traditional style sermon or even take extended communion. Young people today need our training and enabling in the power of the Spirit, to be weavers of new cloth, builders of the new Church of England.

Many young people like small groups or cells where their spirituality can be explored and their own issues debated. These can be peer-led with the vicar or the youth worker acting as supervisor or guide.

Complementing the cell-groups will be large celebrations together. Young people can create the most wonderfully imaginative and God-centred worship. The whole church will find blessing in worship led and composed by young people. We should place much responsibility for the creation of new worship into their hands. Young people love times of sheer exuberance and shouting praise and dancing and waving and being passed bodily over heads and pouring out their very souls in love and commitment and adoration. Huge crowds, exuberant one moment, can be utterly still the next for prayer and devotion. Thousands will suddenly all sit and listen intently to teaching.

The final service of Holy Communion in Lambeth Palace garden at the close of the marvellous 'Time of Our Lives' weekend was one such service. The modern worship of Matt Redman was hand in hand with the uplifting, more traditional, choir leading the 'Hallelujahs.' The huge marquee seemed filled with God's Spirit as cheering, dancing and praise led into the pin-drop still reception of the Archbishop's sermon.

In the recent past, the organ with its power to fill the whole building with sound was the most efficient and up to date way to do church music and so church bands were disbanded. Now other instruments are chosen for their power to fill buildings with sound. Young people have discovered a worship which fills the whole building, be it cathedral or hall. The great pile of speakers and the huge amps are the organ pipes for today. The instruments are those of a modern Psalm 150 plus everything that has breath and electronic wizardry.

Young people have rediscovered the power of symbols and use these so imaginatively through video projectors and compatible computer programmes. Honey may be used to remind worshippers of sweet times and lemon for bitter times. Both sides of the brain are invited to interact. There is a move away from worship that is all words and concepts towards a use of all the senses. One is reminded of Christianity's Jewish roots with its powerful story-telling and use of symbols.

2. *Pastoral Care*

Pastoral care of young people will have to recognize that for many the Church and Christianity are irrelevant. It is no longer an issue which begins and ends at the church door.

Back to School

As we search for imaginative contact points with young people, schools will fill the frame. Several publications demonstrate the potential contact points for a church with today's school population. See, for instance, Nick Watson, *Working in Partnership with Schools* (Grove Books Pastoral Series No 64); David Lankshear, *Churches Serving Schools* (National Society, 1995); *Support Your Local School—A Guide to Opportunities for Church Involvement in Schools* (Schools Ministry Network, 1996)—contact via 207–209 Queensway, Bletchley, Milton Keynes, Bucks, MK2 2EB, Tel 01908–856000. Today's youth culture does not reject Christ, it simply does not know who he is. The church's role in education is very important. Clearly the academic study of faith no longer includes 'believe this—do not believe that' but we might hope that the idea of God is treated with respect, even by non-believing RE teachers. As a church with the privileges of having both church schools and the right to sit on governing bodies, we can surely try to appoint teachers who will teach that the option for theism is just as, if not more, convincing than the option for atheism.

But as the publications referred to above point out, RE is not the only contact point in schools. Christians can be so active within a school community that young people grow up surrounded by people who believe and live out Christian beliefs. The institutional church may be irrelevant but these Christian folk among whom they grow up are definitely not. These people seem kind, caring, real, friendly, helpful, good at listening, fun, interesting. 'There is something about them.'

After-school clubs have been an excellent development as a means of reaching many young people and children who will never be brought to church on Sundays. It is good to market these where possible as joint school/church activities. Youth work post-11 thrives on good work and relationships with the under-11s.

Young Christians from within the school community may be keen, with the support and prayers of their church, to take school assemblies. This is a challenging but powerful witness. It shows that Christian faith is not just for the visiting speaker.

Pastoral care in schools, as well as in centres of further education where there may even be a resident chaplain, provides the church with great opportunities to share love and care. We may have good youth counsellors in the congregation or people willing to be mentors. Several LEAs require the use of such mentors. School's Outreach (Chief executive, Gordon Bailey, 10 High Street, Bromsgrove, Worcestershire, B61 8HQ Tel 01527 574404) model a wonderful pastoral care approach which is school based but spills out into the community of the young person as well. This provides care, which is truly relational and stands with the child at home and in school. Churches sponsor these Pastoral Care Workers who have a base in the school itself. There is a good deal of liaising with the Headteacher before the post begins.

Churches employ excellent full-time schools' workers who often work across a range of schools providing contemporary music for assemblies and lunchtime clubs etc. These workers are usually very skilled in relationships with young people and seem to be very effective in crossing cultural divides with the love of God. Some of these workers are gifted musicians and the loving, healing, challenging voice of God clearly speaks through their songs.

Such workers are usually active in the 'Personal and Social Education' classes where teenage issues are frequently discussed. Here they role model a Christian lifestyle and demonstrate the good sense of it. The power of such role modelling cannot be overstated. Into the arena of young lovers of pleasure and quick fixes, come young Christians who dress and speak youth language, yet live a radical difference. One girl shared with workers how their lesson gave her the courage to do what she really wanted to do—say 'No.'

Especially in schools' work it may not be the vicar who is the best communicator or pastor. We are not only dealing with a generation gap, but with a culture gap. To expect most young people to understand the vicar's role outside of weddings and funerals, let alone sing a hymn or know what a 'collect' is, is way off the mark. Body language is important, as are clothes. Image really matters even if it should not. Yet again the vicar's role is redefined. They become the trainers, not the frontline.

However, what a vicar does have is the social standing and the skills to make quality relationships between senior managers in educational establishments and the church. These relationships will provide the open or shut doors of opportunity for contact with young people. Such relationships should be nurtured with the utmost urgency today. If we are not working at excellent relationships with the local schools we are probably impoverishing the youth work of the church.

School Stress

School is often a good place to be but there will be a special consciousness of exams for many young people. Standard Assessment Tests at 7, 11 and 14 as well as two years of GCSE coursework mean that, at least in their minds, they are very busy with school. I have really found this to be a stress for young people and one that has got in the way of some exciting opportunities. Schoolwork is important. Should it be an obsession? We do have to help young people keep a sense of perspective and a holistic view of education. When, at eleven years, ponies are promised by desperate parents, to encourage (persecute) a child to do well in the exam for the selective school; when a child commits suicide over GCSEs, I want to scream at the system, 'I know exams matter, but they don't matter that much.'

Abuse

Childline has received half a million calls over the last twelve years. In 1998, there were 115,000 first time callers. There are 8,000 long-term callers. The chief issues are: family relationships (13%), physical abuse (11%), other people's worries (9%), and sexual abuse (8%). Boys can be in deeper crisis having waited longer to phone.

The 12–18's age range makes up 62% of Childline callers. The top concern (17%) is bullying. Like many forms of abuse, this is a silent suffering. The terrible loneliness and impotence of the victim, is not helped by a church which fails to recognize the reality of this major concern. Bullying awareness work at church will enable those persecuted to come forward before too much damage is done.

The NSPCC states: 'Each week one child under five dies following abuses and neglect. Each year an estimated 150,000 children are physically abused. 11% of adults report they were sexually abused as children. Each week some 450,000 children are bullied at school. Cruelty to children costs this country over £1 billion every year.'

There are very worrying rising trends of both attempted and completed suicide among young people. Clearly, any church embarking on work with young people today must be very conscious of the 'House of Bishops' Policy Document on Child Protection' and the guidelines and procedures taken from it. Every diocese will have this document and a summary guide to it.

What the Church Can Do To Help
Helpful Pastoring

Church leaders need to offer biblical teaching, to provide a rock-like foundation from which to make wise choices, especially on money, sex, drugs and alcohol. The Book of Proverbs saw these issues as relevant about 3000 years ago. They still are. So why is the institutional church judged irrelevant to these issues? Perhaps young people turned up for two years and heard the full range of *ASB* themes preached. Then they walked. How many of those who preach the *ASB* themes prepare with the needs of young people in mind rather than the needs of older people?

Research demonstrates that young people find teaching and pastoral assistance most helpful when it is understanding, full of listening, encouraging, local, confidential and non-judgmental. Help needs to be ordinary, non-bureaucratic, trusting and relaxed. The church should be well placed to deliver such care. The community aspects of the local parish church or cell group should mean it is very approachable and helpful to its own population of youth. Sometimes young people need professional counselling but often they just need to know it is all right to express emotions and be helped to do it safely. Sometimes all they need is to be heard.

Accompanying

Maxine Green and Chandu Christian in their lovely book called simply, *Accompanying* demonstrate the enormous value in someone being alongside young people as accompanist, friend, guide, listener, advisor.

'One rural parish in Devon, keen to enable young people to develop relationships with older members of the congregation, decided to try out an idea. Each young person was asked to write down two things for which they would value prayer and was then, after the morning service, encouraged to ask an older member of the congregation to take their piece of paper and, during the coming week, to pray for them... After the following week's service, the same young people were encouraged to repeat the exercise and give their slips to the same adults. The conversations that ensued even after the first week were very significant, with congregation members asking 'their' young person how things were in relation to what they had prayed for...

This process enabled some adults to see their role as accompanists, even if for a short time. Their awareness grew out of growing concern initiated by the young people involved.'

Maxine Green and Chandu Christian, *Accompanying* (CHP, 1998)

We will want to pastor, befriend and accompany in ways that are acceptable and helpful.

Listening and teaching need to co-exist. Being willing to learn from people of greater experience is itself something worth learning. Yes, teachers still need to teach and all of us need to learn. I recall wonderful evenings of being with small groups of teenagers as a catalyst for their own discussion. Rather than arriving armed with 'the lesson for today,' we simply relaxed together and discussed (I mostly listened) whatever they felt relevant. There are times to speak and times to listen. It is a great privilege to be trusted by such teenagers to be present as they work out who they are and where they belong. The listener learns too.

I sense, in complex modern living, that such times of listening and being with, are essential. In listening and discussing we can sense the fogs clearing on past, present and future.

3
Who is in Charge?

Leadership and Structure for the Third Millennium
I can remember being slightly shocked once when visiting a church to discover that when the children left for their Sunday School classes, the vicar went with them and left us in the hands of a lay person for the reading, the sermon and the prayers.

A Minister for Youth and Children
Since the demise of the young curate it has usually been the norm that the spiritual care, teaching, counselling and correcting of children and young people has been the voluntary task of capable and committed church members. But the *prima facie* question that we should address is, *'Who is doing the pastoral care of our children and young people and are they the right people?'*

Imagine this situation. Whilst trying to decide upon a residential home for your grandmother you visit one establishment where the proprietor says that he has always loved older people and has always felt that he has had a gift for caring for them. He demonstrates this but has no formal training or qualifications. He admits that he can do a fantastic job assuming that there are no problems, but in the case of any difficulty he would need to consult an expert.

When all is well most of us would be relaxed about leaving the care of someone we love to amateurs. However, in times of special need, we would seek out the experts and find the best possible care available. It is exactly the same with the spiritual care of our children and young people.

With the steady rise in the age of ordinands since the war, churches have increasingly relied on young volunteers to lead the youth work. But with a decline in the number of Christian young people in the 20–40 age bracket that method has become more and more difficult to sustain.

The Rise of the Full-time Youth Worker
Churches who can afford it have sought a solution by employing young people as full-time youth workers. Some have proven themselves as volunteer leaders, some have taken some training at, say, Bible College. These are people who in previous generations would have entered ministry through traditional channels, but more recently these have not been welcoming to them. It is not easy to pinpoint why this is but some are seen to lack experience of life or the right educational qualifications, whilst others are not considered to have a wide enough expertise of different church tradition.

Increasingly, numbers of younger people are seeking formal training through other routes and the new 'Centre for Youth Ministry,' now in its second year, has nearly a hundred students on its books.

As a result there are already 1,200 full-time church-based youth workers or youth professionals, the majority of whom are working in Anglican churches. There are several reasons for this:

- Growing parental concern for their children's spiritual growth and safety
- Decline and changed priorities in statutory youth work provision
- Increased financial resources available from church members
- A desire not to be left behind and not to lose young people to churches that do have youth ministers
- The priority of mission to young people on church agendas
- Lack of voluntary leaders

The particular blend of factors and motivations and the combinations and alliances that lead a church to employ a youth minister vary from church to church. But it is all too common for the churches' motivations not necessarily to coincide with the motivation of the person chosen for the post or the necessity of the ministry required. A full timer may be taken on to mastermind the care of young people who are perceived to be living in a different world—perceived as difficult or beyond ordinary reach of what normally happens within the church. This can result in disagreements about the vision of youth ministry within the church.

Two Common Misunderstandings about the Work of the Full Time Youth Worker
- They are supposed to bridge the generation gap. It is deemed that young people need to have something reflecting their tastes, preferences and language and so a professional is taken on to either be that bridge, or find ways of providing for this generation gap.
- They are meant to prepare young people to be the church of tomorrow. It is felt that as young people live in a different culture, they may need special help to understand practice and worship. They are provided with a separate programme until they are ready and able to join the mainstream of church life. The professional's job is to find ways to educate and integrate young people into the mainstream of church life.

These would be fine (although we might have theological problems with the second, more common way of working) if all that had to be bridged were a generation gap. But the challenge now is of a different order than for previous generations. What we are seeing now with our young people is a cultural era gap rather than a generation gap. The 'gap' is no longer one of young and old when, for instance, one generation liked the Osmonds and another Boyzone. It is the basis upon which such tastes and preferences are chosen that has changed and is still changing. The issue of tastes and preferences is secondary to that of the wholesale transformation of the culture for those growing up now. Young people are an emerging new culture. Acknowledging this change is of crucial importance if we intend to provide pastoral care for young people.

Traditionally churches may have described youth ministry as 'nurturing young people in the Christian faith,' emphasizing discipleship and commitment. Or it may be more 'evangelistic' reaching out and drawing in young people from a fallen world and the dangers of youth culture. Some would rather perceive the thrust of their ministry as 'being salt and light in the community.'

A Historical Perspective

Historically youth ministry has grown out of many different theologies and traditions but has often expressed itself in two major approaches—the youth club and the youth fellowship—and two minor ones—the school Christian Union and 'detached youth work.'

However, despite the best efforts, the old patterns of working are not producing the goods. Youth clubs have become unmanageable in many areas and have been closed. Youth fellowships have been forced to cater for a younger age range and have shrunk in size. Christian Unions are not the force that they were, as many Christian young people will not go near them and so they end up providing lunch-time entertainment rather than Christian input or fellowship. Christian 'detached work' sadly can be so tied up with social agendas and funding requirements that the gospel is almost invisible.

These problems are not just affecting the effectiveness of our outreach but are also reaching right into the heart of Christian families within the church. There is huge anxiety as parents see the children of fellow committed church members abandon their denominational church and sometimes their faith. The sight of a church or programme that they feel will 'keep' their child throughout the difficult teenage years is enough to make them swap fellowships even if they are not themselves comfortable with the change of worship style or theology.

A New Way of Being Young and Christian

Failure of the existing models of youth work has led to a creative explosion in approaches. In addition to the four mentioned above—youth club, youth fellowship, Christian Union and detached work—there are now dozens of potential methodologies around the country. Cell groups, creative arts teams, sports programmes, peer ministry, house groups, after-school Christian clubs, various youth worship forms, social action groups, youth councils and mentoring, to name but a few.

Some of our young people within church will connect with teh approaches traditionally more associated with unchurched young people. Young people outside of church life may, in some cases, respond more effectively to those in keeping with in-house discipleship patterns.

Although once large, the pool of young people with Christian values inherited from their parents and grandparents is declining. Most churches find it easiest to minister to this small pool as it holds similar values. A church may spend increased time, energy and money to try and fish in the pool but will only achieve diminishing returns for its investment. There is a very real danger that the church could come to represent the last bastion of a dying set of cultural values unless it finds a way to fish effectively beyond the pool. Not to move on may leave a church wedded to modernity—offering a meta-narrative of reasoned certainties (be they evangelical or liberal ones), purpose, knowledge and progress but it will be empty.

In a consumer society it is possible for a few churches to target their youth ministry into this declining pool and thus gather a thriving group. When churches try this and are at least moderately successful, they are often consciously or unconsciously perceived as ideal 'models' of what church youth work to be because they are perceived to be successful in reaching and keeping young people of the sort that church expects to see. But it does nothing in Christ's name for those outside the pool. (Indeed it does not do much for those in the pool, as they become part of the church sub-culture which preserves spirituality in a time warp).

The Church—an Exclusion Zone?

Methodologies based upon these two laws leave a growing majority of young people excluded because they cannot connect to the culture of what we are doing and what we are about—the packaging that Christianity comes wrapped in. It is not merely a question of the style of songs in our worship or the choice of the video but a matter of exclusion by the very questions that the work addresses.

Otherwise excellent programmes and ministries are left failing—not because of their quality or the time and effort spent on them but because they are not appropriate. Churches that have unconsciously taken on board the *'successful youth work'* models from others may be left demoralized as similar programmes fail in their area. The style, ethos, underlying presuppositions and expectations are inappropriate and/or the pool of young people to draw from is too small or non-existent.

We may be doing good Christian youth work, engaging the young people we have contact with, developing positive spiritual relationships, empowering them and enabling them to ask spiritual questions—in fact doing everything that we feel we should be doing. But even after all this we can still leave our kids nowhere to go that makes any sense.

A New Way of Being Church for Young People

Discussions about new ways of being and doing church are very much in vogue at the moment. We have to take care that in our good-intentioned efforts to provide something for young people that is accessible and what we might call 'modern,' we are not perpetuating something that is of our world and not of theirs. The ethic behind our new services and events is often straight to the point—we need something that is culturally appropriate for our young people because our church is not, and we need to get them in.

It is difficult for youth workers. We are anxious because our programmes do not seem to be connecting with the young people's cultural world. We are anxious because the pressure is on to get young people into church—to validate our existence, the resources spent and also because churches are getting older. Our work is often a 'results' and 'justification' cycle. What we need is support for our work that gives us freedom to experiment with new methods and the freedom to fail without the guilt. Where that permission is given and resources granted, youth ministry is moving from events within existing structures towards a concern with church planting into postmodern culture. This is evidenced by the rise in culture-specific worship in its various forms: from multi-media service to alternative worship; from five in a front room to five thousand in a big top. Many of these are the result of the eruption of Christian faith in and out of the new culture.

If we believe that God by his Spirit is actively missioning in the world then surely this is what we should expect and be looking to encourage. As co-workers with Christ our role is to engage with what he has already indicated. We need to train our young people in leadership of the peer group, provide them with a share of resources, give them our love and support and enable them to operate as the church from within their culture.

Is a Postmodern Church Post-Anglican?

Obviously the answer to this depends upon our understanding of Anglicanism. Some things inherent to our understanding of 'Anglican' will inevitably disappear in the transition to a postmodern world, especially some of the agendas attached to the battles of the past. If we equate Anglicanism with a 'Christian faith for the people,' expressing itself in ways that the community can understand and which is committed to God's kingdom mission to all, then postmodern need not mean post-Anglican. Styles of worship and the appearance of church may change but at core, many of the values of what is Anglican will be seen to be present still.

In reality much of the space for new developments in worship has been (surprisingly) created by the Anglican church: allowing not just physical time and space with buildings but liturgical space to be inventive and try new things and even theological space to explore what things might mean.

Looking back at recent patterns in youth work we can guess that many new forms will come into existence, but over time only a few will survive. Within Anglicanism, some of the postmodern expressions of church will become dominant forms (like the *Soul Survivor* model of youth congregation) others will become minority preferences and yet others will be temporary transition points to something or nothing else. The nature of culture is such that in the foreseeable future there may not be a unifying style or rite but rather a series of creative sources bubbling up and spreading with different influences in different cultural groups and personality types.

New Patterns of Leadership for a Postmodern Church

How can we begin to change structures and patterns of leadership to create the best environment for continuous growth?

If the Anglican Church is to survive in England it must rapidly establish congregations, cells and programmes into the new culture. Much discussion is going on concerning the format for youth congregations, patterns, structures, worship and so on. But what about the leaders?

We have talked about youth ministers as church planters, worship leaders, programme planners, cross-cultural representatives and missionaries but who else may find that they share some or all of these roles and responsibilities?

The seventeen-year-old leading a cell group?
The nineteen-year-old gap year student giving 'Time for God'?
The twenty-two-year old leading a worship group?
As well as the twenty-five-year-old youth minister responsible for a monthly youth congregation of four hundred young people.

How Should Leaders be Trained, Recognized and Accredited?

Consider this example. A church pays to employ a youth leader. They are a young and enthusiastic person with a call to serve God, lots of potential but no real training. After several years the monthly youth service evolves into a weekly youth congregation of a hundred and fifty young people which the youth leader is effectively pastoring. He or she is a youth minister. In one sense this is brilliant—but consider the implications:

- Who does the youth minister answer to when they have been in ministry for longer than the vicar let alone the curate?
- What are their resources and support to judge if something new is heresy and where it fits into theological tradition or historical practice?
- What happens regarding baptism or, more problematic, communion?
- Where does the youth minister go for help and support when a young person dies or the worship leader is found to be sleeping around?
- What happens when the youth minister has a personal or faith crisis?

We need to be more ready to embrace a less hierarchical, more team orientated method of working. Strategies of development could be long term rather than based on a two- or three-year youth ministry contract. As character as well as gifting is recognized, training would be best appropriately delivered in a form that could ensure continuous professional development across parishes. Clericalism in the form that we know it may be one casualty of the transition to postmodern church.

We need to create the freedom to fail. Those being innovative on the edges of the edges of the culture need to be free from the constraints of having to produce 'results.' We can imagine this as a youth ministry freehold—where it is safe to develop new styles of youth worship and ministry and also to make mistakes and fail in the short term because the long-term gains are so much greater. These gains are not simply numerical ones and are sometimes very hard to judge. They are the postmodern styles and forms of church that may be the mainstream as we move into the first century of the new millennium.

We need built in accountability and supervision. We need to identify and train those who can be the equivalent of Rural Deans and Archdeacons to pastor the youth ministers.

Other Dilemmas for Emerging Leaders of Young People

Youth ministry is perceived by many as a preparation ground for 'proper' ministry to the 'proper' church. The youth minister's role is not really a full ministry (compared to that of a curate, a trainee with responsibility for young people). This view sells youth leaders and young people short.

Firstly it can leave young people feeling pastorally insecure. As one young person said, 'I told X my thoughts and problems and they left; then I told Y what had happened to me and then they left. Why should I share anything with another youth minister?'

Secondly it sells young people short by saying that it is all right to give them the second best. The message put across is 'Practise on the young people and when you are more experienced, work with adults.'

This view also sells our youth ministers short. Not only can a church fail to understand the nature of their minister but also they can fail in giving the necessary support and training.

We have a new generation of ministers who minister to those aged under 25. This is the growing army of full-time parish youth professionals. Rarely they are ordained, occasionally they are licensed, sometimes they are accountable to the diocese but more often they are not. They are sometimes under-qualified and mainly unacknowledged and unaccredited by the wider church and yet they may be more influential over the lives of future church leaders than anyone else.

Some Key Areas for the Emerging Youth Ministers
1. There is a question of resource allocation. At present 80% of clergy are over forty. We need a much fairer spread of stipendiary ministers. It could be argued that, because most of us come to faith by the time we are 20 we need a disproportionate number of full time youth and children's workers. We need to be thinking about appointing fewer clergy to a dying current church and more to the new. One way of doing this would be to transfer stipendiary posts from vicars to youth ministers.
2. Training therefore has to be transformed. Many young leaders have had to endure the 'snakes and ladders' models of training whereby before you may climb a new ladder you may have to slide down the snake from the top of the previous ladder that you climbed and then start all over again. We need to see theology as something we do as we minister rather than something that is done to us before we can minister.
3. Ministry is a long-term commitment for many. What is the recognized route that people are expected to take? In other words what is the equivalent in youth ministry of what is known as 'career development'?
4. Much of our vocational assessment is geared to looking for future potential—we need to find new ways of assessing the ministry of practitioners now, bearing in mind that their ministry will change and develop in the future in different ways.
5. There needs to be a nationally recognized accredited role that youth ministers can be part of. Whether this takes the form of a permanent diaconate is an argument for another place. However, the situation where youth ministers are preachers, teachers, leaders of worship and designers of liturgy into a new culture while being excluded officially from such ministries in the old culture is an anachronism which needs remedying.
6. A transfer of financial resources for training so they are more equitably shared between preparing for ministry to young people and preparing for ministry to adults. Why do those who minister to the young have to find the money to pay for their own training while those ministering to older people do not?

We need to be as inventive in our ways of recognizing, accrediting and training the leaders of the emerging church as the leaders have been in engaging with the new culture. If we fail we will continue to fall short of providing adequate pastoral care to the growing numbers of young people whose only real opportunity of a meaningful connection with Christianity will be through these emerging patterns.

4
What Shall We Do Now?

'We set aside our seeker strategy and intensified our eclectic style of Anglo-Catholic liturgical cues, Pentecostal rock-n-roll rhythms, high-tech segues, Reformed preaching, and Quaker collectiveness (both the silent and participatory varieties) and all this in a 200 year old Congregational meeting house…'[1]

We can either be despairing or look at the signs of life, hope and change which are talked about in these chapters. God is re-creating his church. We live at one of the most interesting and challenging times in the history of the church in England and the Church of England. Some will witness it; few of us will lead it. But let us encourage it all we can as we see the birth of 'emerging church.'

The information in this Grove booklet is sufficient to indicate that unless the Anglican Church is to be reduced to a tiny exclusive eucharistic sect, we have to appreciate the urgency of the task. It takes ten years for a five-year-old to become a peer leader. It takes ten years for a peer leader to develop into a full-time minister. Given the urgency of the task what can we do practically?

1. Look at your own church. How many young people each year celebrate their 18th birthday and are part of your worshipping congregation? What challenge does this bring to you?
2. Start a ten-year plan for your own church based on your five-year-olds and your fifteen-years-olds. (Or if more appropriate, your new-borns and your ten-year-olds.)[2]
3. If you are a minister and if you believe the gospel must be passed on to

---

1   http://www.christianity.net/leadership/9L2/9L2037.html (Quoted in Paul Roberts, *Alternative Worship in the Church of England*, Grove booklet W 155, Cambridge, 1999).
2   See Penny Frank and Geoff Pearson, *Too Little-Too Late! Children's Evangelism Beyond Crisis* (Grove booklet Ev 41, Cambridge, 1998).

the next generation, decide to spend at least half your ministerial time and effort in supporting and managing work with young people. See it, if you like, as investing in the future.
4. If you are a lay person, take a look at what happens in your church and local area then help to rebalance the budgets to ensure youth and children's evangelism is made a priority. (The 1991 census figures are rather out of date now but you could see how the ages profile of your community and your church compare and then target the 'gaps.')
5. Consider taking on a 'gap year' young person, or postpone that building project in order to pay someone to do some youth work.
6. If you are a bishop, follow the 1998 Lambeth Conference recommendation to bishops of sitting down and spending time with young people.
7. Go to your deanery and then diocesan synod and propose that any money saved from the reductions in clergy goes to ministry to young people. (At least one diocese is already doing this).
8. Plead for the capping of the numbers of places at ABM conferences for those over 40 thinking of stipendiary ministry—and a fast track selection process for those under 30 until the imbalance in age profile has been corrected. Go to your synod and propose this.
9. If you have a local ordained ministry scheme, check what the policy is regarding keeping the age profile fair and balanced.
10. Find out who the Bishop's ABM selectors are for your diocese and spend an evening with them finding out how they do their job and ensuring that they know the kind of youth ministry which is developing nationwide. Talk to your Bishop about the criteria for selection in the diocese and ABM. Do the criteria for ministry take account of the need for people committed to mission and evangelism especially among the young?
11. Be even more radical. There is talk about changing ordination training to make it more on-the-job and integrated. Lobby your bishop and any others you think might be able to influence matters.

Jesus said,'Let the children come to me and do not stop them, because the Kingdom of heaven belongs to such as these' (Matthew 19.14). Roll on the millennium generation! Let us begin to hand on pastoral care and worship to them.

For further reading, see George Lings, *Eternity—the Beginning*, Encounters on the Edge No 4 (Church Army) and Patrick Angier, *Changing Youth Worship* (London: National Society/Church House Publishing, 1997).